POWER MACHINES

POWER MACHINES

KEN ROBBINS

Henry Holt and Company ◆ New York

The author wishes to thank the following owners and operators of heavy equipment for their cooperation and goodwill:

Ed Thompson, Sr., of Duffy Thompson Contracting; Charlie Grimes, the owner of Grimes Contracting; Frank Alfieri of Alfieri Contracting; David Paolelli, the superintendent of sanitation, town of East Hampton; Dave Brown, Barry Forde, and Bob Greene of the East Hampton Town Highway Department; Jim Peters, media officer at the Long Island Lighting Company and Jim Brennan, plant manager at their Northport, New York, generating station; Kevin Gershowitz of Gershow Recycling in Medford, Long Island; Ray Smith, Roland Roosa, and Jack Brophy of Eastern Tree Service; and especially Jody Friend of the Springs Tree Service.

—K. R.

This book is for Gregory Bernard.

Henry Holt and Company, Inc., *Publishers since 1866*
115 West 18th Street, New York, New York 10011

Henry Holt is a registered trademark of Henry Holt and Company, Inc.

Copyright © 1993 by Ken Robbins
All rights reserved.
Published in Canada by Fitzhenry & Whiteside Ltd.,
195 Allstate Parkway, Markham, Ontario L3R 4T8.

Library of Congress Cataloging-in-Publication Data
Robbins, Ken. Power machines / by Ken Robbins.
Summary: Photographs and text describe such work-saving
machines as a crane, jackhammer, bulldozer, and backhoe.
1. Machinery—Juvenile literature. [1. Machinery.] I. Title.
TJ147.R55 1992 621.8—dc20 92-30649

ISBN 0-8050-1410-1 (hardcover)
3 5 7 9 10 8 6 4 2
ISBN 0-8050-5297-6 (paperback)
3 5 7 9 10 8 6 4 2

First published in hardcover in 1993 by Henry Holt and Company, Inc.
First Owlet paperback edition, 1997

Printed in Hong Kong

First Word

Power machines are awesome. They are bigger than we are, they have more strength than we do, and they can work harder and longer than we can, too.

Power machines are being used right now to build roads, clear land, or dig foundations. They are hard at work all the time—moving, crushing, pulling, lifting, scraping, spinning.

They are what we build to make the jobs we do easier. Power machines do what we do, but on a much bigger scale.

Scoop and Dump

A payloader is used to move very heavy things—huge loads of earth or gravel or garbage. The bucket at the front of the machine is as big as a large car. It can lift more than six tons. A payloader can push or drag, but it is particularly useful when a load needs to be raised high in the air before it is dumped. A payloader is often used to load heavy materials onto large trucks.

Lift and Place

Some heavy objects, like bricks, would break if they were just dumped the way a payloader dumps gravel. A forklift is designed to pick up a stack of heavy items, move it, and set it down gently again. This one runs on propane gas and can pick up almost 3,000 pounds. Forklifts are very nimble—they can really zip around in tight spaces—so they can be used both indoors and outdoors.

Raise and Lower

When heavy objects have to be lifted higher than a forklift can reach, it's time to call in a crane. Think of a crane as a giant fishing rod. A very strong steel cable hangs from a steel boom the way a fishing line hangs from a fishing pole. Whatever is to be hoisted is fastened to a hook at the end of the cable. A powerful winch (like the reel on that fishing rod) winds the cable up, bringing the object with it. In these pictures a crane is being used to raise huge slabs of marble to the top of a skyscraper. This crane can lift 25,000 pounds at a time.

Toss and Churn

Mix cement, sand, gravel, and water together and you have concrete. Concrete must be carried in a transit mixer so that it doesn't dry and harden. A transit mixer is a truck with a big, round revolving tub. The tub spins around, tossing and turning and mixing and churning about twelve tons of those ingredients while the truck is on its way to a building site. When the transit mixer arrives, a worker opens up a gate and lets the concrete pour out into molds, perhaps to make a foundation for a new house. When the concrete dries, it will be as hard as rock.

Smash and Crack

Anyone who has ever fallen down on a concrete sidewalk knows just how hard it is, but a jackhammer can bust up a concrete sidewalk in a matter of minutes. A big, very loud engine called an air compressor drives a pointed steel blade up and down hundreds of times per minute. One worker aims the blade and operates the machine. The force is enough to smash up even the hardest concrete.

Crush and Grind

When big buildings are torn down or old sidewalks are torn up, a concrete crusher turns the huge pieces that are left into piles of sand and gravel. A payloader dumps large chunks of concrete into the crusher. Then—almost the way our back teeth grind up crunchy food—gigantic steel rollers grind them into sand and small bits of gravel. The sand and gravel can be used all over again in new buildings and roads.

Push and Pile

A bulldozer is a very powerful earth-moving machine. Like a tank, it moves on steel treads instead of wheels. Like a snowplow, it pushes everything in front of its steel blade—earth and trees included. Bulldozers are used to clear the land of trees and shrubs for a building site. They can also flatten hills and fill up valleys, changing the very shape of the land for a new road.

Skim and Scrape

When building a new road, a road grader smooths and levels the earth after a bulldozer has done its work. As the grader travels over the ground, it drags a blade that evens out the rough surface of the earth, making it flat enough to pave over and drive on.

Hum and Spin

This giant machine is just one of four steam-turbine generators that make electrical power at a power plant. Each one is bigger than a house. In gigantic boilers that are six stories high, one and a half million gallons of fuel oil are burned each day to turn water into steam. That steam spins the turbines in the same way that flowing water turns a waterwheel. Each turbine, going around 3,600 times every minute, turns a generator. Finally, those four generators together transform all the mechanical energy into 400,000 kilowatts of electricity—enough to light up all the lamps and run all the appliances in 240,000 homes.

Pull and Transport

Driven by an engineer who sits in its cab, a locomotive is the engine that pulls a railroad train along the tracks. This one is a diesel engine. It can pull up to twelve passenger cars at speeds of up to sixty miles per hour. That's more than 186,000 pounds per car, or 2,232,000 pounds in all. Locomotives that are built to pull freight trains can pull much more weight—up to a hundred cars or more—but they go more slowly.

Dig and Plant

Planting a small bush or a single bulb is easy. Just dig a little hole and put the plant in. But moving a tree that was planted maybe a hundred years ago and is already thirty feet tall—for that you need a tree spade.

First, the four steel blades of the spade dig a hole where a tree is to be planted. The operator uses the machine to pull out a plug of earth and put it aside. The hole and the plug might be five feet across and five feet deep. Then the same blades are used to dig up another plug of earth, this one including the tree, roots and all. The tree spade moves back to where the first hole was dug and lowers the tree into it. When the planting is done, you would hardly know that the tree hadn't always been there. The plug of earth goes back in the hole where the tree originally was, and the landscape is hardly disturbed at all.

Dig and Dump

For digging really big holes in the ground or deep trenches, nothing beats the backhoe. With its long reach and huge bucket, it works like a giant arm. This particular backhoe runs on treads like a bulldozer, and the whole machine can twist around or swivel to dump its load on any side.

Squoosh
and Squash

When automobiles can't be driven anymore, they are recycled. Anything useful or not made from metal is removed. A car flattener does the rest. It presses down on the empty car with 85,000 pounds of pressure per square inch, squashing a normal-sized car into a pancake about fourteen inches thick. Eventually, that pancake of metal will be melted down and used to build new cars.

Last Word

We haven't always had power machines, and for many centuries people got by without them. To truly appreciate power machines, try to imagine how we would do the jobs that the machines do if we didn't have them, and all the ways the world is different because we do.

Power machines can do amazing things because they are so big and so incredibly powerful, but for the same reason they can be dangerous, too. That's why the men and women who operate them have to be very skilled and extremely careful. Never get too close to a working machine.